A LASTING TRANSFORMATION VOL. 1

Your First Thirty Days

Albert Cabrera

ISBN 979-8-88943-309-5 (paperback)
ISBN 979-8-88943-310-1 (digital)

Christian Faith Publishing
832 Park Avenue
Meadville, PA 16335
www.christianfaithpublishing.com

Printed in the United States of America

To my Lord and Savior, Jesus Christ—my strength. my fortress. my helper. To my future wife, Katherin, who gave me my life back. Thank you for challenging me into becoming a better man. It's God, you, and me against the world. I love you always.

Very truly I tell you, whoever believes in me
will do the works I have been doing, and they
will do even greater things than these.

—John 14:12 (NIV)

INTRODUCTION

The Lord said to Moses, "Come up to me on the mountain and stay here, and I will give you the tablets of stone with the law and commandments I have written for their instruction."

—Exodus 24:12 (NIV)

God is calling you on to the mountain. There you will receive instructions and directions. Listen to His voice. He has a work, a mission, an assignment that will change you and your generation. Quicken yourself—.

You are a dreamer, a visionary. You have a great calling. You have been impregnated by His Spirit for a great purpose. It's time to birth it. You are here for that very reason. You were created for God's glory (Isa. 43:7). God deposited within you the gifts, and talents, and the anointing needed to thrive in this life. You cannot wait any longer. This generation is waiting. Do not doubt. You have it within you.

You should be a teacher by now is Hebrews 5:12, "Although by this time you ought to be teachers, you need someone to reteach you the basic principles." Often we need a reminder and a guide to help us activate the gifts and the anointing God has given us through His Holy Spirit. This book will be your guide. God has given me the opportunity to write this book with you in mind. Though the main idea of this book is to encourage believers to become entrepreneurs, the principles contained within are biblically sound and can be applied to ministry.

Our church pews are occupied by gifted, talented, and anointed people; but they are dormant—people who feel the desire, the yearning for more, but feel stagnant. This book is for you. Exodus 31:3 reads, "And I have filled him with the Spirit of God, with wisdom, with understanding, with knowledge and with all kinds of skills." You are equipped by His Spirit. It's time to awaken that power.

You are gifted, talented, and anointed. You could no longer allow time and life to pass you by. Your family, your community, your ministry, your businesses are waiting for you to birth the vision. You must pour out to this generation what God has poured into you. Activate your drive and your willingness to succeed. It's time to make your footprint. Let us go on this a journey together.

Invite the Spirit of God to come with you. Use this time to draw nearer to God. Pray and meditate on the scripture assigned with every chapter. Remember the words of Jesus in John 15:5: "I am the vine; you are the branches. If you remain in me and I in you, you will bear much fruit; apart from me you can do nothing." Your life will never be the same. Are you ready?

Take heed of Proverbs 16:3: "Commit your work to the LORD, and your plans will be established" (ESV).

VISION

Where there is no vision, the people perish.

—Proverbs 29:18 (KJV)

Can you imagine a world without direction? An idle humanity with no drive, not knowing left from right, a world without discoveries, no technological advances, no advances in medicine, and no clear pathway to the future—humanity will cease to exist. Therefore, vision is important.

A lack of vision will cause the people to perish.

The verse continues by stating that those "that keepeth the Law, happy are they." God's word is our moral and day-to-day compass. It clarifies our vision, and without it (God's word), we will perish. The psalmist said His words are a "lamp onto our feet," keeping us from stumbling.

The vision we will discuss is not physical sight, but the ability to project where you want your future self to be. When you can see within your mind and within your heart a pathway to achieving your dreams and goals, that is vision. Vision is having direction. Vision is unlimited, unselfish, unrelenting—it has no end.

Well-executed vision will create a legacy, a blueprint for others to follow. It allows future generations to reach greater heights than the previous. Where do you want to be in five, ten, or twenty years? Can you see it, that place of achievement? Whether a preacher, singer-songwriter, pastor, musician, Sunday school teacher, youth pastor, outreach ministry, missions—whatever it maybe—your vision is for the masses. Write down your vision and make it clear, clear enough that others can follow it. Habakkuk 2:2: "Then the LORD answered me and said: 'Write the vision And make it plain on tablets, That he may run who reads it.'"

Get ready to impact the world.

DAY 1

Self-Discipline

Success can be measured or defined in various ways. What are your metrics for success? How do you measure success? Is your idea of being successful based on material gains such as cars, homes, jewelry, or other material possessions? Or is it based on the quality of people that surround you, family, and friends. Your idea of success can vary depending on your values, but it cannot simply be about money. Money is a tool, a resource. As a tool, money can be used to provide for our loved ones. As a resource, it can be used to bring forth new opportunities. But it should never be the driving force of our passion. 1 Timothy 6:10: "For the love of money is the root of all evil: which while some coveted after, they have erred from the faith, and pierced themselves through with many sorrows" (KJV).

The Bible doesn't teach that wanting money is bad, but loving it is. The Bible teaches the importance of good money management, good stewardship. We must be good stewards in the little before given access to the much. We all want to be at the top of the mountain, the summit. Getting there will require great sacrifice. The climb is difficult, but the conditions at the summit are harsher. The air is thinner, the winds are stronger, and the climate is much colder at the top. You must fight harder to remain there.

Your dream must have a greater purpose than just making money. Don't misunderstand me; money is very important. Money gives you access to many opportunities. But what gives money its value is what you do with it. Most of us are amazed by the personal stories of self-made millionaires or billionaires. They began with what it seemed absolutely nothing but achieved great success. Your vision, your dream will finance your future.

We are impressed with the likes of Bill Gates and Jeff Bezos of the world. Though it may seem as if they have always been on top, I can assure you this is not the case. Microsoft and Amazon began in incredibly small scales. Both had to overcome incredible amounts of obstacles. I'm sure the thought of quitting entered their minds; but they believed in their dream and they believed in their product, even though at times they could not believe in themselves. Bill Gates struggled with personal confidence. He told a group of students at Harvard, "Even the idea that Microsoft would be a big company, I never would admit that to myself."

You are not alone in feeling fearful and doubtful; it is human nature. But we must overcome fear and doubt. If not, they will paralyze us. Over time, Microsoft and Amazon became two of the world's most powerful companies, making Bill Gates and Jeff Bezos two of the richest men on the planet. Success will come at its due time.

There is no substitute for hard work, but you must also work smart. I can't tell you how many times I failed, how many times I felt lost, desperate, and depressed. Every time I thought the sun was about to shine through, a gray cloud appeared. I had dreams, I had goals, and I thought I had a clear vision. The problem was not the obstacles; it was not the lack of time and knowhow—it was a lack of discipline. Until I realized that I was my worst enemy, I remained stagnant. I lacked organization, drive, and self-discipline. Something had to change (more like *someone*), and it was me.

I began to take small steps on the right direction, which over time transformed my life. Your life is about to change for the better. I want to join you in this life-changing journey. Be strong and steadfast. You must commit yourself to this challenge. Don't skip a day and don't cut yourself any slack. Don't try to cut any corners either. Follow through with the daily activities. At the end of this journey, you will welcome the new you.

Remember, in the next 50 days, we will be creating the correct behaviors to help you succeed in life. This book is not meant to be a fix-all but instead to motivate you and help you along the way. But if you seriously commit, you will be on your way to a better, stronger, more determined you. Though it can take anywhere from 18 to 254 days to develop a habit, the key numbers seem to be between 60 and 66 (https://jamesclear.com/new-habit). This is where *A Lasting Transformation Vol. 1* comes in—a guide to aid you in getting to the mountaintop and prepare you to thrive there. Let's make success your new habit. Let's jump right in.

What Is Self-Discipline?

Merriam-Webster defines *self-discipline* as (1) "correction or regulation of oneself for the sake of improvement" and (2) "the ability to make yourself do things that should be done." I like the terms *correction* and *regulation*. The road to success is seldom a straight line. You will face many forks in the road, different paths from which to choose. Correcting and regulating our thought process is the first step to self-discipline. Change your mindset. Train your mind to think about success instead of defeat. Change your vocabulary. Turn the "I can't" to an "it's possible." Surround yourself with positivity. Before you convince the masses, you must first convince yourself. Proclaim that you can, and you will achieve it. "Whether you think you can, or you think you can't—you're right," Henry Ford said.

Day 1

Self-discipline will help you get the job done. When others are quitting, you will be determined to make it to the finish line. We must learn to focus. I believe in this formula: self-discipline × time = focus. Zero in on the goal like an archer aiming for the bullseye.

Keep your mind on task. Eliminate distractions. Keep your emotions in check. As humans, emotions are a huge part of who we are. But we must not be controlled by emotions. Emotions are not constant, and they can be deceiving. Rationalizing emotionally will get you into trouble. Can you remember an occasion when you argued in favor of your emotions, only having to apologize at the end because your emotions led you to believe you were on the side of righteousness, but once rationality kicked in, you quickly realized you were wrong? This can be embarrassing. Therefore, we must regulate our emotions. When our circumstances get tough—which they will—you can champion through it. Let's self-improve by replacing bad habits with new good habits. We must correct one bad habit at a time.

We will identify three bad habits that are major roadblocks to success. Let's start with a huge dream killer—disorganization. If you are a disorganized individual, it's time to get organized. Clutter is usually the sign of a disorganized mind. Our thoughts and actions most be systematic. Don't confuse an analytical mind with a cluttered mindset. How do we break this bad habit and become organized and mentally fit? Let's start by writing things down. According to the article titled "Neuroscience Explains Why You Need to Write Down Your Goals if You Actually Want to Achieve Them" on Forbes.com by Mark Murphy, you are 1.4× more likely to achieve your goal if you write it down. Self-discipline is the difference between the successful and the unsuccessful. Write down your goals, your dreams, your vision and develop a road map with checkpoints.

Checkpoints will help you assess how far you've come and give you a good picture of what needs improvement. Also, checkpoints will provide insight on the resources needed to get to the next checkpoint. Your goals must be realistic. Simply writing down "I want to make a million dollars" is not enough. How are you going to earn these million dollars? Be more specific; it does not have to be perfect at the beginning but be clear.

For example, if you have a gift for literature, if you love writing, a simple goal can be "I'm going to be a *New York Times* bestselling author." Find a niche to write about. Use your talent. Remember, everything you need to succeed is in you; you are simply training yourself.

Invest time developing your gifts and your talents. Don't settle at the level you are in right now. When properly managed, your gifts and talents will increase. Do you recall the parable of the talents in

Matthew 25:14–30? God is the Master in this story. He has entrusted you with talents. Put them to work. The servants that invested their talents received an increase, but the servant who hid his talent was stripped of everything. Your anointing, gifts, and talents will open doors to new possibilities.

Define where you want to be, short term and long term. Once you have a clear vision on where you are headed, get ready to fight for it. You might also say, "I'm not sure what my dream is or where I'm headed." This journey should set you on the right path or at least put you on the right track. Once your goal is written down, let's create an action plan. What are the necessary steps to achieving this goal? Create a step-by-step roadmap. Ask yourself, *Do I need more training in my area of interest? What resources do I need?*

Reality check

If you need more training in ministry, go get it. If personal finances are currently a burden, search for the most cost-effective options. Bible colleges and seminaries are great institutions for learning, but tuitions cost can be high. Do not create a financial hole for yourself. Try a cheaper option. Enroll in an accredited Bible institute. Accredited institutions are held to a higher standard and may ease the credit transfer process. (If you decide to obtain a higher education degree, of course, situations vary and colleges have different credit transfer policies. Do your research.) Speak to your church leader; ask for a recommendation. Many accredited Bible institutes have great curriculums with a lower price tag.

Many believers are gifted as stewards. The Holy Spirit has imparted many with the wisdom to create and manage businesses. Whatever area it maybe, seek the proper training. Follow a pattern of organization. Being organized gives you a sense of pride and a sense of direction. Organize your workspace, your living space. First impressions are still important. Do not show your potential church member or clients (if in business) a disorganized workspace. Let your guests see that you take pride in your work and that you respect them by keeping things in order.

Bad habit number 2: Procrastination

We are all guilty of this. The invitation to speak was made two months ago, but you prepared the night before. You know you had a deadline. You had one month to prepare the report, but you did it the night before. You know you had to study for the exam, but instead you watch the football game. It's time to take things seriously. Take your goals seriously. Remove whatever is causing you to waste valuable time. Instead, invest it into your destiny. Invest two dollars and purchase a weekly planner. Plan out your day the night before. Set your schedule and stick with it. Schedule your leisure time, but don't overdo it. When it's time to work, it's time to work.

Eliminate distractions

The twenty-first century is filled with things fighting for your attention. You must wisely decide where to invest your time. Time is your most valuable asset. Time is too precious to waste. We must learn to invest time, not just simply spend it. Before you invest a large portion of your time, ask yourself, *Is it beneficial to me? How would it improve my life? Can this potentially harm my progress?* You must be the hardest worker in the room. There is time for everything, but you must keep it within a schedule.

The next fifty days are meant to challenge you. When you feel that you are about to hit a breaking point, remember that diamonds are formed in extreme pressure and heat. Weight trainers will tell you that for new and stronger muscles to grow, the old muscles need to be torn. We are training our most important muscle and that's the brain. You will get better at it. You will get stronger. Stick with it.

Bad habit number three: Stop dwelling in failure

Remember, the mind is the battlefield. As a soldier preparing for war, so too must we prepare. We have all faced disappointments, and truth be told, we will continue to face disappointments. Life comes at us hard, but we must hit back harder. Self-discipline will help you overcome disappointments.

Maybe it was not the outcome you expected, but life is not over yet. You can pick yourself back up and give it another go. Before you can convince anyone to believe in you, you must first convince yourself to believe in you. It sounds like a cliché, but you must believe in yourself. You are a powerful force, placed on this earth for a reason.

When a wall appears, you must become a wrecking ball and smash through it. Don't dwell on past mistakes. Don't see them as failures but teaching moments. Success will not come overnight. No matter what your personal definition of success is, it will take hard work. The winning formula is this: self-discipline + good strategies + time = success. Apply yourself to these three things, and it will produce success.

Today's Activity

Organize yourself. Plan out the next seven days. Divide your time wisely, include your work schedule, personal engagements, self-enrichment sessions, and leisure time.

Scripture of the Day

Genesis 1:1–2

In the beginning God created the heaven
and the earth. And the earth was without form,
and void; and darkness was upon the face of the
deep. And the Spirit of God moved upon the face
of the waters.

Though the earth was formless and void and darkness was upon the face of the deep, the Spirit of God moved upon the face of the waters. Today, you may feel empty, formless, and void, covered in darkness; but rest assured that the Spirit of God will move in your favor. Call out to Him—He's listening.

Day 2

Whatever It Takes
Develop a Business Plan
and Follow Through

Behold, I have given you authority to tread on
serpents and scorpions, and over all the power of
the enemy, and nothing shall hurt you.

—Luke 10:19

What are you willing to sacrifice? What price are you prepared to pay to achieve your dreams? Success will not look for you. Success has no friends. It will not knock at your door. You will have to get up early every single morning and pursue it. Success has an entourage that will stand in your way. You will have to wrestle and subdue each one to take hold of it.

You will encounter fear. Fear is part of the human condition, but to conquer fear is godly. We need to rise above the limitations we have created in our minds. Fear will try to paralyze you. It will try to consume every aspect of your life. What do we do when we are at an all-out war with fear? We fight. We read in Deuteronomy 31:6, "Be strong and of good courage, do not fear nor be afraid of them; for the LORD your God, He is the One who goes with you. He will not leave you nor forsake you" (NKJV).

The antithesis of fear is bravery

We must be brave. *Bravery* as defined by *Merriam-Webster* is "the quality or state of having or showing mental or moral strength to face danger, fear, or difficulty." Bravery is not the absence of fear, no. It's understanding what's at stake, looking at fear right in the eyes, and getting the job done.

This reminds me of the biblical story of David and Goliath. Whether you consider this to be simply folklore or true events, there is a great lesson to be learned. In 1 Samuel 17, the Bible tells us a story about a giant from Gath. As the author begins to describe Goliath, we cannot resist the urge of amazement at the giant's physical attributes.

According to the Bible, Goliath was six cubits and a span in height (roughly under ten feet tall, depending how you define the cubit). But wait, the story is not about the giant—the story is about David, the young shepherd boy. With an entire Israeli army paralyzed with fear at the sight of this adversary, David meets the giant Goliath at the battlefield and challenges him. Goliath charges toward David, and David charges toward Goliath.

Reality check: maybe you are telling yourself that the obstacle you are facing is bigger than you, and maybe it is. But there is nothing bigger or greater than your God. Your determination to succeed makes the difference. Set your mind on Go. Say to yourself, "There is too much at stake. My family, my home, the ministry, my career, my dream—they are all at stake." Rise against fear. Not in my house!

Fear understands one very important factor. Fear knows that you and only you can defeat it. How? The moment you convince yourself that you will get through it. Visionaries understand what's at stake. Visionaries will not back down at the sight of adversity. Visionaries understand that their footprints are a pathway for the next generation to follow and achieve greater feats. David was a visionary. He understood that the victory God was giving him that day will directly affect the next generation. (Read 2 Samuel 15.)

As the story narrates, the giant seemed more physically able and better prepared for the battle, but David's faith and determination made the difference. Don't mess around with fear. When you knock fear down, don't wait for it to get up. David hasted toward the fallen giant and with the giant's own sword beheaded Goliath. He fought against fear and conquered it.

Your journey to success will cost you everything. It will not be easy, and that's all right—we don't want easy. Things that come easy are momentary, but the things that cost you everything will be everlasting. What price are you willing to pay? Are you willing to get up at four in the morning? Are you willing to invest all the necessary time to your craft so you can achieve your goals? Are you willing to put in the work to self-improve? Are you willing to fight through the pain? Are you willing to fight through the tears? Listen, it is okay to cry, but is not okay to quit.

Understand this and train your mind on what I'm about to tell you. Being tired is never a good excuse to quit. Your goals don't care if you're tired. Opportunity will not wait for you. Let's get into a warrior's mentality. Fight through the fatigue, through sickness, through doubt, and through despair, understanding that you are not fighting in vain—seeing, tasting, and knowing that sooner rather than later you will take hold of success. What are you willing to sacrifice? The routine of working late, planning, executing, day in and day out, getting up early every day like clockwork.

Having a well-defined vision, direction, projection, a blueprint for your goals will create passion. This is a fire burning deep within, telling obstacles to get out of your way. You do not have a second to lose. Your mind is set on winning. Are you willing to pay the price? I know you are. I believe in you. Let's make it happen.

Today's Activity

Step 1. Write down your ideas. Write them down as they come; you can organize them later. Remember, dreaming big is extremely important; but in the beginning stages, it is also important to be realistic. You are going to start small but will scale up. Once you're comfortable with the ideas you have written down, start to organize them.

Step 2. Create an outline. Outlines can be very simple. Don't over-complicate it. With your idea as the header, list the resources needed to make your idea a reality. Include the fiscal amounts that you estimate that will be needed for each step. For each bullet point, create a deadline. Hold yourself accountable. Use your outline to create your business plan and model. Your business is an extension of yourself. Invest the time. Work hard at it. I don't necessarily agree with you quitting your current job just yet. You will need capital to fund your business, and your bills at home need to be paid.

Step 3. Time to do some market research. Are there any similar businesses in your area? In other words, who's your competition. If your idea is unique—which is not always the case—get to work on it. If there are other similar businesses in your community, do not fret. Even if you share a niche with another business or businesses, you can always bring something fresh to that market. Once your research is done, go back and make any necessary changes to your outline.

Step 4. You need a business location. Some entrepreneurs start right from home, but if you decide to rent a separate location, beware of the cost. Consider the cost of rent, utilities, equipment, employees (if applicable), materials for the product, and the general costs of doing business. Therefore, I recommend starting at a small scale, and as the business progresses, you can scale up.

Step 5. Deciding on a name. At this point, if you don't have a name for your business, it's time to choose one. Try to keep the name simple but memorable. Depending on the complexity of your business, you can register it yourself with your state or if you don't feel comfortable, hire someone to do so. The requirements to legally register a business can vary from state to state, so check with your state.

It is important to check with your state because licenses and permits maybe required. Once you have successfully registered your business with your state, get an employer identification number (EIN). You can obtain your EIN number directly from the IRS, and it's free of charge. Make sure you know your legal type. Not all business types are created equal. You may need to complete additional forms with the IRS. Check the IRS website for instructions.

Step 6. Accounting. You will need to either purchase accounting software or hire someone to keep your books. You need to be organized. You can purchase a do-it-yourself accounting software, and as your business grows, you can delegate that responsibility to an accountant.

Step 7. Gather your team and market your business. As the CEO, you need people as driven and disciplined as yourself to make it work. In the beginning, it may just be you; but you can only occupy one place at a time, so you will eventually need a team. Once your team structure is set, let's go market your business. Sign up for events in your community such street fairs, conventions, and or other social gatherings. You must put your vision out there. People need to know that your business exists, and it has a great product to offer. Social media is such a powerful tool to achieve this. Use all the available resources. All these steps will take time. Do the research, put in the time, and be steadfast but also be patient.

Scripture of the Day

Genesis 1:28

> And God blessed them, and God said unto them, Be fruitful, and multiply, and replenish the earth, and subdue it: and have dominion over the fish of the sea, and over the fowl of the air, and over every living thing that moveth upon the earth.

You have been given dominion. Dominion is control. The dominion Adam and Eve lost due to sin, Jesus Christ gave back to us. God has given you authority. Use it for His glory.

DAY 3

Invest Your Life into Something Worthwhile

Even every one that is called by my name:
for I have created him for my glory,
I have formed him; yea, I have made him.

—Isaiah 43:7 (KJV)

You were created to bring God glory in everything you do. Your ministry is for His glory, not social status. Even your business is for His glory. Remember that your vision is for the benefit of many. Every day ask the Lord how you can bring Him glory through your business venture. Don't forget that it is God who produces the growth.

"The two most important days in your Life is the day you were born and the day you discover why," as the saying goes. The day you discover your purpose is the day you will tap into your real potential. Your business and or area of ministry should be something your passionate about.

Today start thinking about the business name. Write down a few name ideas. The name should be short and memorable. The largest companies in the world use very short business names, usually one word. Look at these examples: Apple, Amazon, Twitter, Walmart,

Target, Staples, etc. Your business name should stand out but simple enough for your potential customers to remember.

Scripture of the Day

John 1:4–5

In him was life, and the life was the light of men. The light shines in the darkness, and the darkness has not overcome it.

Jesus is the light of the world. He is our light. He will guide us through the darkest times. Today is a great day to thank Jesus for who He is—loving, kind, merciful, and all powerful. Darkness will never overcome His light. You are in good hands.

DAY 4

See Yourself There

For as he thinks in his heart, so *is* he. "Eat and drink!"
he says to you, but his heart is not with you.

—Proverbs 23:7 (NKJV)

Visualize it. Can you see yourself there? To say perception is important is an understatement. Perception is the ability to see and comprehend the elements around you. Have you ever heard of the metaphor of seeing the glass have empty or the glass have full? You must find the positive in situations, no matter how difficult they may seem. Easier said than done, you say. I hear you, but it's possible.

You will face diverse challenges throughout your life and career. Each challenge will present you with an opportunity to learn and grow. Even if the challenge or situation seems negative, you can learn something from it. Financial hardships teach us to build a nest egg— emergency savings—to save for the unexpected. If it's a separation, divorce, or breakup, without tearing yourself down or resting all the blame on your shoulder, you can learn what areas you were neglectful, areas where you can improve in your next relationship and possibly even salvage the broken one.

Today, start behaving like the minister or business owner that you are. Develop a professional demeanor. Read as much as you can to improve your vocabulary. Analyze your moves and organize your day. Let's be more fiscally responsible—give to God what belongs to God and to Caesar what is of Caesar. Create a budget and apply it. Pay all your bills on time and try to live under budget. Find areas within the budget where you can save.

For example, when short on funds, instead of going to the movies, go to the park. Find areas in your budget where you can save and place that money in a high-yield savings account. I recommend an online savings account. Online high-yield savings accounts usually offer higher interest rates. Even though it may take a business day or two to get your funds, HYS's are a great alternative to traditional banks. Make sure the online banking institution is FDIC insured and the services are offered by a reputable company.

Scripture of the Day

Matthew 5:3

Blessed are the poor in spirit, For theirs is
the kingdom of heaven.

The term poor in spirit does not refer to material poverty, it refers to a humbleness, a meekness. We can't ever forget that we need God. Only through His grace and power can we achieve greatness. Jesus said that the humble are blessed, because the kingdom of heaven will be theirs. What an awesome promise.

DAY 5

Don't Say "I Can't," Say "It Is Possible"

I can do all things through Christ who strengthens me.

—Philippian 4:13 (NKJV)

Because of Christ, you are unstoppable. In your weakness, His strength is made perfect in you. Change your vocabulary. Words are not carried away by the wind. Words are heavy. Words will stick. Words can change your mindset. "The power of life and death is in the tongue," we read in Proverbs 18:21. Today, begin to change the visual and auditory messages that enter your mind. Read more scripture. Study the biblical principles found in scripture regarding business. We want to please God in all we do. Keep your mind on Him and your goals.

Isaiah 26:3 says, "You will keep *him* in perfect peace, *Whose* mind *is* stayed *on You,* Because he trusts in You" (NKJV).

Listen to motivational speakers. Read motivational books. You don't have to spend money on these books as of now; go to your local library. It's free. A word to the wise, return your library books on time.

Today's Activity

Narrow down your possible business names to three. Try to visualize these three remaining names in your company's marketing materials. Which one of these names stand out the most? Remember to keep the business name as short as possible. This can be applied in ministry as well. Try to keep your ministry name as short as possible as well, to avoid using acronyms. Short ministry and business names are easier to remember.

Scripture of the Day

Matthew 8:27

But the men marveled, saying, what manner of man is this? that even the winds and the sea obey him!

Jesus is in control. He has power over every storm. Run to Him. In Him you will find shelter from every storm. Ask Jesus to cover you and your family every single day.

DAY 6

Decisions, Decisions

Trust in the Lord with all your heart, and do not lean on
your own understanding. In all your ways acknowledge
him, and he will make straight your paths.

—Proverbs 3:5–6

What is your decision-making strategy? Remember, you are now thinking as a business owner. You cannot make rash decisions. This also applies to ministry. What steps do you follow when deciding a big purchase for the ministry or church. Who do you consult before making the decisions? These are very important questions that can save us heartache and money in the long run.

Develop a decision-making strategy. For example, use a pros-and-cons list until you become an expert in decision-making. Always think about the short-term and the long-term implications of your decisions. Think long-term gains rather than the short term. Which do you prefer, fifty thousand dollars now or a hundred thousand dollars in sixty days?

Today's Activity

Develop a decision-making method. Think of a decision that must be made right now. Whether a personal and/or financial decision, right down the pros and cons, the short-term and long-term implications, and try to make the right call. Decision-making is an art. It's a skill you will continue to develop. You will not be 100 percent accurate, but you will minimize mistakes.

Scripture of the Day

Proverbs 15:22

Without counsel, plans go awry, But in the
multitude of counselors they are established.

Scripture teaches us to restrain from hasty decisions. Seeking counsel, especially on life-changing decisions, can avoid a deluge of problems. The heart can be deceiving. Your heart can be steering you, pushing to make a quick decision, but don't do it without counsel. Seek God's counsel and the counsel of God-fearing people. God will establish your plans according to His will.

DAY 7

Invest Your Time Wisely

I must work the works of him that sent me, while it is
day: the night cometh, when no man can work.

—John 9:4 (KJV)

Time is your most valuable asset. I will say this repeatedly.
God the Creator is unlimited and eternal in nature. He
lives outside the constraints of time. He's not affected by it; eternity
abides in Him, according to Isaiah 57:15. He is from eternity past
and will forever exist.

We are his wonderfully made creation. Made in His own image
and likeness. But our existence is governed by seasons, as ordained
by the Creator. He blessed us with the gift of time. Not all receive
the same measure. It may be decades, years, months, or mere days. It
doesn't matter. What you do with your measure of time, will give it
its value and meaning.

Reality check: We do not know how much time we have left.
No one knows. We have life expectancy data that gives an estimate
on how long you may live, but there is always the unexpected. Start
by making smalls steps that will lead you on the right path. Start
with a to-do list. Label the priority from low, medium, to high. Write
down who is responsible for completing the task.

Today's Activity

Visit your state's secretary of state website to learn the requirements to register your business or ministry. Don't register yet but learn about the requirements. Requirements will vary by state

Scripture of the Day

Psalm 139:16

Your eyes saw my unformed substance; in your book were written, every one of them, the days that were formed for me, when as yet there was none of them.

Even before you were born, God knew you. He has ordained a plan for you. At times it may feel less than perfect, but it is perfect. The pain makes us stronger; the lack teaches us to cherish, and the occasional feeling of abandonment reminds us to value His presence. God will be with you every step of the way. He has seen your future, and it's going to be great.

Tell the Obstacle, "I Will Break You Before You Break Me"

For I am the LORD your God who takes hold of your right
hand and says to you, do not fear; I will help you.

—Isaiah 41:13 (NIV)

A Warrior's Mindset

Do not be afraid of the voyage. There will be obstacles with everything worth having. Look at obstacles and challenges differently. The obstacles and the challenges are not meant to stop you but to make you stronger. Yes, you will cry, you will scream, your knees will weaken, but you must keep moving forward. Your best life is about to begin, if you defeat the obstacle.

Today's Activity

It's a great day to decide on which business classification you will be filing under. The most common are a corporation, a limited liability company, or even a sole proprietorship. Each comes with its own advantages and disadvantages. Most entrepreneurs elect limited liability company for the protection of personal assets that the sole proprietorship does not offer. If you will be immediately seeking for investors, the corporation structure will probably benefit you best, as investors prefer this business structure.

Scripture of the Day

Psalm 119:71

It is good for me that I was afflicted, that I
might learn your statutes.

There is no losing in God. We may be broken at times, but God will rebuild us every time, if we seek Him. We lean on the promises we find in scripture. Hold on to His promises, which are *yes* and *amen* in Jesus Christ who loves us.

DAY 9

God Wants You to Succeed

For I know the plans I have for you, declares
the LORD, plans for welfare and not for
evil, to give you a future and a hope.

—Jeremiah 29:11

Good planning, self-discipline, perseverance, patience, and time will produce your breakthrough. Breakthroughs don't automatically happen; they will not come on their own. You must fight for your breakthrough. Every success story has one thing in common—difficulties. Don't for a second think that because you are facing difficulties you are not cut out for this. It's the complete opposite. Your difficulties will become a testament of your greatness. The difficulties and struggles will condition you for the mountaintop.

Today's Activity

If you have decided on your business name and your business structure, visit your state's secretary of state website and complete the articles of incorporations form to register your business with your state. Keep in mind that filing fees vary from state to state. Other things to consider before filing—will you be the only member listed in the articles of incorporation? Will you have officers, treasurer, and a secretary? Who will be your registered agent?

As explained by Legalzoom.com, an LLC registered agent is an individual or entity which has been designated by the LLC to receive service of process notices, government correspondence, and compliance-related documents on behalf of the LLC.

Scripture of the Day

Genesis 9:16

Whenever the rainbow appears in the clouds, I will see it and remember the everlasting covenant between God and all living creatures of every kind on the earth.

God has not forgotten His promises—He remembers. At times we feel as though He has no memory of us, perhaps He is preoccupied with the affairs of the world and we are last on the list. I assure you, He remembers His promises. Do not lose faith. He will come through for you and your family.

<h1 style="text-align:center">DAY 10</h1>

See Your Worth

I praise you because I am fearfully and wonderfully made;
your works are wonderful, I know that full well.

—Psalm 139:14 (NIV)

I strongly believe that mankind is the most fascinating organism on this planet. Our minds and bodies are incredibly complex. We have discovered so much yet know so little. The technological advances in the last century are astonishing. From gazing at the stars, to walking on the moon, to the breathtaking views beyond our solar system—we have come so far and, yet we are merely discovering ourselves. That is the point. We live in a galaxy with billions of stars, trillions of organisms, but there is only one you.

You can't be duplicated; you can't be replicated. You are unique. You are not just another life-form using up valuable resources. You are here for a reason. You have a message that the world needs to hear. You have a voice that will be heard loud and clear through your actions. You have a lion's roar within you, ready to be let out.

Volcanoes are an extreme force of nature, so powerful that they have destroyed cities. I think history's most famous volcanic eruption was in the year 79 AD in Pompeii, Rome (the Roman Empire at that time). Mount Vesuvius erupted, and thousands lost their lives. It was truly a catastrophe. The immense pressure building under the surface cannot be sustained forever. Volcanoes need to release this pressure. Can you see where I'm going with this?

Your dreams have been under extreme pressure, with all sorts of attacks to deter you from your goal. I need you to listen. You will not be held back any longer. You have too much to impart in others. You are a teacher, a counselor, a visionary, and a man or woman on a mission.

So they left you, abandoned you. You didn't see that coming. Listen to me, you are still here. Time to bounce back. I speak from experience. I know it hurts. I can understand the emotional, physical, and mental distress that comes with a divorce, separation, or breakup. Stop crying over spilled milk when you are about to buy the whole farm.

I realized that we tend to focus solely on the worth of the individual that is leaving but not on our own worth. We zero in on what they brought to the table. We fall into this pattern of distorted thinking. We believe the lie that life somehow cannot go on. Listen to me clearly—life goes on. Life will not wait for you or for me to get our emotions in place. Life will not play fair. Life is waiting for the opportunity to knock you down. But you will not relent.

Know your worth. Remember the mountains you had to climb to get to this point, the valleys you had to traverse, the deserts you had to experience, the cold, the uncertainties, the tears—everything you had to endure—and you are still here. Know your worth. You are an overcomer. Your value cannot be given a number or price. In this universe, there is not another you. Know your worth.

Have you heard the analogy of diamonds? Diamonds are created from coal. Extreme heat and pressure turn the coal in to a diamond. You are turning into a diamond. You are about to shine; in fact, you are shining already. One important lesson is that a diamond reflects light. It does not carry its own light. Your dreams, your vision, your goals, your destiny—that's God's light reflecting from you. Let that vision shine right through you. Let that goal shine. Let that dream shine! The world needs to hear what you have to say, but don't use your mouth, use your actions.

Today's Activity

Focus on the bigger picture. Take thirty minutes and write down the message you will bring forth to society through your company or ministry. Your company is an extension of you. Writing down your message will give you a sense of identity and direction. Remember, only you can tell your story correctly. Shine on!

Scripture of the Day

Philippians 2:13

For it is God who works in you, both to will
and to work for his good pleasure.

Meditate on this. We are God's vessels, each designed for a specific purpose. God wants to use you. You are His instrument. He is using your life to create a beautiful melody. He takes great pleasure in you. Go on. Let Him use you for His glory. That is our purpose. In this we will find joy.

DAY 11

Rules of Engagement

Do not forsake wisdom, and she will protect you; love her, and she will watch over you. The beginning of wisdom is this: Get wisdom. Though it cost all you have, get understanding.

—Proverbs 4:6–7

Become an expert at the rules. Use the rules to your advantage. Every state will have its own set of laws to govern business. Learn these laws, rules, and regulations. Learn about any permits and/or certifications required to carry out your type of business within your state. Learn about your business tax obligations with the state and the federal government. You don't need to be afraid about your business taxes, just prepared. Once it's time to file, you can seek out a tax professional who can help you. There is do-it-yourself software for tax preparation, but it's always a good idea to seek the counsel of a professional.

Remember, good financial record keeping is your best friend. Keep your receipts for every transaction that involves your business. This also applies to ministry income and spending. Every purchase, every service paid for, income, expenditure, and miles traveled for business purposes need to be recorded. Become a student of deductions. Knowing what you can deduct and claim in your taxes can save you hundreds, if not thousands, of dollars. Learn the tax code for your nonprofit ministry.

Today's Activity

Invest forty-five minutes in choosing your bookkeeping and recordkeeping methods. Will you use software or will you be manually keeping your financial records? I personally like the automation of bookkeeping software. Some of these software companies give you access to their mobile version or apps for your phone, which can be very helpful in keeping track of receipts and miles traveled for business purposes.

Scripture of the Day

1 Corinthians 14:40

But all things should be done decently and in order. (ESV)

Let us honor God in all we do. Let us be good representatives of Christ. We do not walk in the counsel of the wicked. This includes questionable business activities that can damage our family's, ministry's, business's, and our reputation as a believer. Even if men are not watching, God is watching. His desire is for us to do right and live righteously.

DAY 12

Quiet the Negative Voices

Do not be misled: "Bad company corrupts good character."

—1 Corinthians 15:33 (NIV)

Thinking and analyzing are great, but overthinking can be your downfall. Silence the naysayers. It is your God-given vision. Only you have the mental capacity to understand it in its raw beginning stages. Do not get discouraged when others tell you that you can't make it. Unfortunately, so many people can't find the courage to lift themselves out of their pit, so instead, they decide to drag others down. Surround yourself with positive people, like-minded individuals who will push you to become better.

Today's Activity

It's a good day to analyze to whom we are lending our ears. Remove the toxic folk from your life. Partner with people who believe in you and will invest in you. Both nature and nurture will shape you. We create an environment for success when we are among people who share similar values and drive. Always remember that God must be at the center of it all.

Scripture of the Day

Psalm 1:1

How blessed is the man who does not walk in the counsel of the wicked, Nor stand in the path of sinners, Nor sit in the seat of scoffers! (NASB)

DAY 13

Control Your Emotions

He who is slow to anger is better than the mighty, and
he who rules his spirit, than he who captures a city.

—Proverbs 16:32

Think rationally, not emotionally. Keep your emotions under control. We will always make mistakes. That is part of the human experience. Don't breakdown at every mistake or failure. See them as moments of learning. Preparedness and readiness will minimize your mistakes. Most businesses (even so churches) fail, due to a lack of preparation. This includes a comprehensive business plan. Do not dwell in the past. Your idea was good; it probably failed because it was not accompanied with a good plan of action.

Remember, we will be in constant contact with people. We must be patient, loving, and empathetic with others just as God is patient, loving, and empathetic with us.

Today's Activity

Do some market research. Find two or three companies with a similar vision to yours. These are some of your competitors. Write down at least five things that your competitors are doing correctly and five things that they are not. Write down how would you improve on each item listed.

What improvements will you make in the way your competitors engage with customers? Are your competitors neglecting a specific demographic where you can take advantage of? It's very important to ask yourself this question: Why should a potential customer choose me over my competitor? Always find ways to improve yourself and your business.

Scripture of the Day

Mark 12:30–31

"Love the Lord your God with all your heart and with all your soul and with all your mind and with all your strength. The second is this: 'Love your neighbor as yourself.' There is no commandment greater than these." (NIV)

Love your neighbor as we do ourselves. Sounds like a tall order. In a society that teaches us to "look out for number one," we can easily forget this commandment. Jesus loved us so much that He came as a man to reconcile us back to God. He suffered for us when He was innocent. Jesus said in John 15:13, "What greater love is this, that one who gives his life for a friend."

Every day we need to ask God to help us love our neighbor as ourselves, seeing past their imperfections as God sees past ours, even loving those who are difficult to love. There is nothing stronger than love. Where everything else fails, love makes a way.

DAY 14

The Story Is Just the Beginning—It's Not Over Yet

"Forget the former things; do not dwell on the past. See, I am doing a new thing! Now it springs up; do you not perceive it? I am making a way in the wilderness and streams in the wasteland."

—Isaiah 43:18–19

We are entering the second week of the challenge. Go on, give yourself a quick pat on the back. Great! Now let's get back to work. I'm sure by now you have battled with thoughts of quitting, searching for excuses, trying to cut yourself some slack. Don't give up. You have much more to give. The following quote comes from Jesse Itzler's book *Living with a SEAL*: "The 40% rule is simple: When your mind is telling you that you're done, that you're exhausted, that you cannot possibly go any further, you're only actually 40% done." Keep pushing.

Today's Activity

Let's investigate banking for your business. There are so many financial institutions competing for your business. This is a good thing. This means you have more options that can benefit you. A good idea is to find a bank near you that is offering free business checking or a low monthly account balance. Find a business account that is low on fees and gives you cashback options. You probably won't have much start-up cash, so try to save in every possible area.

Scripture of the Day

2 Corinthians 4:8–9

We are pressed on all sides, but not crushed; perplexed, but not in despair; persecuted, but not forsaken; struck down, but not destroyed.

Remember the diamond—pressure on all sides but not crushed. God is our strong tower. He will fight for you. He will lift you up every time. You are not forsaken; you are loved.

DAY 15

Be Bold and Brave

David also said to Solomon his son, "Be strong and
courageous and do the work. Do not be afraid or
discouraged, for the LORD God, my God is with you.
He will not fail you or forsake you until all the work for
the service of the temple of the LORD is finished."

—1 Chronicles 28:20

Your willingness to take risks and the ability to follow through will set you apart from your peers. Consider all the opportunities you've missed due to fear or hesitation. Fear is natural; it's part of our defense mechanism. Fear is a warning signal to help you discern a possible dangerous situation but is not meant to paralyze you. Push forward. God will make your steps swift and meaningful.

Today's Activity

Write down all the equipment, materials, and start-up cash needed for your first day of business. Notice how I did not list "personnel" because most likely, you are the only employee thus far. But if you need to include personnel, go right ahead. If applicable, include payroll for your personnel. Make a detailed list of all equipment dedicated to your business. This list will become your inventory. Add a cash value to each item. Create another list on how much start-up cash is needed and describe exactly how you will spend these funds.

In the beginning, you can feel overwhelmed with all the responsibility as a new business owner. You will have to cover a lot of ground on your own. Remember to invest time in yourself as well. Take time to rest and recharge. Your best life is waiting.

Scripture of the Day

Genesis 13:14–17

And the Lord said to Abram, after Lot had separated from him: "Lift your eyes now and look from the place where you are—northward, southward, eastward, and westward; for all the land which you see I give to you and your descendants forever. And I will make your descendants as the dust of the earth; so that if a man could number the dust of the earth, then your descendants also could be numbered. Arise, walk in the land through its length and its width, for I give it to you."

Your future is secure in God. His plans is greater than you could have imagined. He will expand you in every direction. You will be blessed. Your children will be blessed. There is a land prepared for you and your future generations.

DAY 16

How Bad Do You Want It?

Prepare your work outside; get everything ready for
yourself in the field and after that build your house.

—Proverbs 24:27

How do we define a winner's mindset? That killer instinct that
gets the job done in the crucial moments. In the world of
sports, it is known as being clutch. Your family, your team, your customers are counting on you to get it done.

Discipline yourself to deal with frustration. Instead of shutting
down, being discouraged, or frustrated, look at the obstacle as an
opportunity to shine. Your family looks to you for answers because
your dependable. You are a guiding light. Your team looks to you for
guidance because they have seen you in action. Your team understands that at the crucial moments, you will roll up your sleeves and
get the job done.

Come on! How bad do you want it? Trust in the gifts, the talents, the skills you have developed over the years. How bad do you
want it? Remember all the sacrifices you have done to get to this
moment, this crucial moment. How bad to you want it? It's time to
muster up all your strength and get ready to run through the obstacle. You will not allow obstacles to bring you down; you'll break them
before they break you.

The following are five qualities found in the book *Clutch: Why Some People Excel under Pressure and Others Don't* by author Paul Sullivan. According to Paul Sullivan, all clutch businesspeople possess these five qualities:

1. *The power of focus.* What an awesome concept. You cannot perform at your best if you are distracted. Cancel out all the unnecessary mental clutter. Silence the negative voices and zero in on the goal. Remember, you won't get to the goal unless you put in the work.
2. *The practice of discipline.* Discipline = focus + time, my favorite formula for discipline.
3. *The ability to adapt.* Challenges will change. Even challenges you faced before will appear in different apparel. Learn to see things from a different perspective.
4. *Being present.* You must show up for the fight. I had a teacher in high school who drilled this in our heads; "80 percent of the battle is showing up." Stop missing important meetings. Stop hiding from the problem. Show up and show up strong and ready. Show up ready for war.
5. *The use of fear and desire.* I truly believe our biggest fear should be becoming contempt. If this happens, everything will lose its meaning, and you will lose your passion. Don't become contempt.

There is more to achieve, higher mountains to climb, and you can always expand your legacy. Remember, your vision is eternal; it has no end. Keep focused and keep growing. How bad do you want it?

Today's Activity

Write down how having a successful business will change your and your family's life. Let that be your driving force. Getting it done and understanding why—the purpose of it all—will be your compass. Don't forget that you are building a legacy that will remain long after you are gone.

Scripture of the Day

Matthew 5:14

"You are the light of the world. A city that is set on a hill cannot be hidden."

DAY 17

Enrich Your Mind

Gold there is, and rubies in abundance, but lips
that speak knowledge are a rare jewel.

—Proverbs 20:15 (NIV)

Nourish your mind. Read and study. Become a disciple of the science of success. Seek knowledge. Seek wisdom. Speak knowledge. Speak wisdom.

Today's Activity

We have a two-part challenge. Think about this question: *Are there any degrees or certifications in my business field that will set me apart from my peers?* A degree and certification might be a requirement in your business field by your state, but it can also give you more credibility. If your business field doesn't require a degree or certification, are there any free classes you can attend to sharpen your skills?

The two-part challenge: Research which degrees or certifications are needed in your business field. Do not feel discouraged if you are required a certification. Invest the time and get certified. Follow through. The investments you make in you now will pay dividends in the future. Schedule and attend a free class or seminar to further increase your knowledge of your business.

Scripture of the Day

Ecclesiastes 7:12

For wisdom is a defense as money is a defense, But the excellence of knowledge is that wisdom gives life to those who have it.

DAY 18

Train the Body, Protect Your Temple

Do you not know that your body is a temple of the
Holy Spirit, who is in you, whom you have received
from God? You are not your own; you were bought at
a price. Therefore, honor God with your body.

—1 Corinthians 6:19–20

It is no mystery that your performance in all areas of life is affected by your health. It is important to eat healthy and enjoy a good's night sleep every night. Eating healthy and exercise improves your brain function. According to the article "Regular Exercise Changes the Brain to Improve Memory, Thinking Skills" by executive editor of the *Harvard Health Letter* Heidi Godman, exercise helps with memory, reduces inflammation, and improving overall brain functionality.

Do you desire for your body to perform at its best? Give it the right fuel. Eat a healthy diet. God has given us an amazing temple to watch after. Your body is where your spirit and soul reside. The Spirit of God abides within us as well. Let us honor the house that the Spirit calls home.

Today's Activity

Invest thirty minutes to develop an agenda. Organize your week. Include time sessions for your business, school (if needed), rest and relaxation, exercise, and time to get enough sleep. If you believe you are doing all the right things and still don't feel at your best, seek a healthcare professional. Your family needs you at your best, and so do we.

Scripture of the Day

For while bodily training is of some value, godliness is of value in every way, as it holds promise for the present life and also for the life to come.

—1 Timothy 4:8

DAY 19

Train Your Soul

Praise the Lord, my soul; all my inmost
being, praise his holy name.

—Psalm 103:1 (NIV)

Today's Activity

Gratitude—feel grateful. I understand you have faced many challenges, struggles, and lacked many things. But you are still standing. You are here, and you are about to reach new heights. So many have fallen and have never gotten back up, but you did. Nothing can stand in your way. Time to push harder than ever before.

Take a moment and be grateful. Appreciate all that God has done in your favor and know that He will continue to be by your side. Above all things to be grateful for, be grateful for His salvation. To be great, you must be grateful.

DAY 20

Money
Time to Invest

Wealth gained hastily will dwindle, but whoever
gathers little by little will increase it.

—Proverbs 13:11

Time to see money for what it is—a tool. Money is a resource and a tool that can give you access to great things. Money is not everything; it is a powerful tool to help you enjoy life. Our goal is not only to help you become a successful entrepreneur but also to help you build wealth.

Today's Activity

Find a place where to invest some money. We want you to have a safety net. You don't need much to get started. You can get started with as little as twenty-five dollars. If low risk is your investment method, try high-yield savings accounts and/or bonds. If you are a little riskier, try stocks. Remember, these are for long-term.

Dedicate a small portion of your earnings on a weekly, biweekly, or monthly basis to investments. There are investment apps that allow you to enter the stock market with very little funds. Reach out to a financial adviser that can analyze your unique circumstances and help you decide.

49

DAY 21

Be a Voice of Hope

Not looking to your own interests but each
of you to the interests of the others.

—Philippians 2:4 (NIV)

Let your vision be a light to others. Making positive contributions to humanity is a mission in which we must all share. Your company's interaction with its clients should be more than business related. Create a faithful following.

Today's Activity

This is a good one. Invite at least five people to a focus group about your company. I know this can make you feel a bit vulnerable, but if you want your customers to faithfully follow your company, you must listen to them. Create a ten-minute pitch. The pitch should be straight to the point and clearly define your products or services. Develop a short questionnaire for the group. Ask the participants what they thought about your products or services and what products or services they would like to see. This information will give you a keen insight into your customer's mindset. Let us know how your focus group experience was. Your success is our number one priority. Send us your story to Albert.katherinconsultants@gmail.com.

DAY 22

It's Not All about Us—Let's Share

Whoever is kind to the poor lends to the LORD, and
he will reward them for what they have done.

—Proverbs 19:17 (NIV)

By now you should have received your articles of incorporation from your state. If you have not, visit or call your state's secretary of state's office and inquire. Now is time to get your employer identification number from the IRS. The good news is that it is free.

Follow the instructions in the IRS website. If you are having trouble obtaining your EIN, send us a message and we will help. It is very important that you know your company's filing structure before you apply for the EIN. If you are using a corporation structure, know the difference between C-corp and S-corp. S-corporation designation is a taxation election. S-corporation is not another form of corporation; it is for tax purposes. S-corp owners or shareholders will have a pass-through taxation. This means that any profits or losses will be reported in the individual's tax return.

Today's Activity

Today's activity is optional, but I believe this activity will be one of the most important thus far. Donate twenty dollars to someone in need. If you don't have twenty, donate ten, five, or even a dollar but donate. God will remember you in your times of trouble.

Share what you have learned thus far with a relative, friend, or neighbor who is struggling. Let's speak life to everyone around us.

Challenge Yourself

Do your best to present yourself to God as
one approved, a worker who has no need to be
ashamed, rightly handling the word of truth.

—2 Timothy 2:15 (ESV)

We can always push ourselves a bit further. I particularly love challenges. Challenges will help you grow.

Today's Activity

Sign up and participate in a community event. A marathon is a good idea. Plan for the day. Don't show up unprepared. Give yourself enough time to prepare. If it is a marathon you sign up for, train for the event. Create special business cards. Socialize. Use the event as a platform to engage others and present them with your product and services. Feel free to share the love of God at the event.

If running is not your thing, sign up for a different event. But I recommend you doing something out of your comfort zone.

Your Moment Will Come

Wait for the LORD and keep his way, and
he will exalt you to inherit the land; you will
look on when the wicked are cut off.

—Psalm 37:34

Positive results will begin to happen. Don't give up. You are creating a lasting empire. This is not a get-rich-quick scheme. Time to start thinking about marketing. With today's technological advances, you have a vast array of affordable marketing resources. You can advertise in social media such as Facebook. Many companies offer affordable do-it-yourself website design platforms and business cards and will even set you up with online merchant services so you can accept payments on your website.

Today's Activity

Do some research on do-it-yourself website-building platforms. It's important that you don't strain your budget. Things to keep in mind: Most of this service providers will charge you a monthly fee, so you will need to purchase a domain name (about twenty-five dollars per year), and you will need to invest an ample amount of time in creating your website. Or if your budget permits, you can hire someone to create the website for you. Design your website with these three elements—elegance, modern, and ease of navigation—for your customers. Reach out if you need any assistance with your website development.

Day 25

I Know It Hurts but Get Up!

"Have I not commanded you? Be strong and courageous.
Do not be afraid; do not be discouraged, for the Lord
your God will be with you wherever you go."

—Joshua 1:9 (NIV)

Winston Churchill once said, "Success is not final, failure is not fatal: it is the courage to continue that counts." Failure is not fatal. It's not going to be an easy climb to the mountaintop. The road to success is paved with hard work. You must put in the work. If you stay the course, you will achieve greatness.

Let's raise some money. Whether it is for inventory, marketing, or prognosticated expenses, you will need start-up cash. The amount of start-up cash can differ greatly by your business type. For example, a freelance writer may need less startup cash as opposed to an individual starting a landscaping business.

There are different ways you can raise money for your business. Two of the most common ways are through investors and business loans. Most investors and banks will require you to have a comprehensive business plan. Let us begin to create your business plan. We are going to take the next few days to create your business plan. I don't want you to get overwhelmed, so we will take it step by step.

Today's Activity

Create an executive summary. An executive summary is just that—a quick summary of your business. Do not make it complicated. Try to keep it just under two pages. Some experts do recommend that when creating your business plan, leave the executive summary for last. I recommend at least a rough draft of the executive summary at the beginning of the business plan creation. Keep your executive summary simple but elegant. This is the first—and sometimes the only—part of your business plan banks and investors will look at.

Your executive summary will need to cover the following seven areas:

1. *Your business idea.* In two or three sentences.
2. *Your services or products.* Don't overdo it. Only list your main services and products.
3. *Your goals.* List your short-term and long-term goals for your company.
4. *Your target clients/customers.*
5. *Your market research overview.* Who your competition is and what are you going to do better than your competitors.
6. *Your team.* Who comprises your team and what strengths they bring to the organization. This includes education and expertise in the specific business field.
7. *Your finances.* The last section is reserved for your business's financial picture. If you are seeking financial support, this is where you want to list it. Be specific. Specify how much you need and a detailed breakdown on how you will use the funds. We are here to help you through this process. Contact us at albert.katherinconsultants@gmail.com.

DAY 26

Dealing with the Unexpected

To everything there is a season, and a time
to every purpose under the heaven:
A time to be born, and a time to die; a time to plant,
and a time to pluck up that which is planted;
A time to kill, and a time to heal; a time to
break down, and a time to build up;
A time to weep, and a time to laugh; a time
to mourn, and a time to dance;
A time to cast away stones, and a time to gather stones together;
a time to embrace, and a time to refrain from embracing;
A time to get, and a time to lose; a time to
keep, and a time to cast away;
A time to rend, and a time to sew; a time to
keep silence, and a time to speak.

—Ecclesiastes 3:1–7 (KJV)

How do we deal with the unexpected? Well, the short answer is preparation. Your business needs to be ready for a slowdown in sales, a fire, equipment malfunction, and so many other scenarios. Creating a financial safety net is key. Build your business savings to help you navigate the unexpected.

Today's Activity

Part two of your business plan is to describe your company. Again, keep it simple but elegant. Describe your mission statement. Describe your vision and your company's beliefs. With a little more detail, describe your company's goals. With a bit more detail, describe your target client/customer. Describe your business field or your industry. What's the forecast for your industry? Is growth in the forecast or stability? What's your business legal structure? Is it a partnership, corporation, sole proprietorship, or an LLC? List the owner(s), shareholders, and members, if it applies.

Greatness Is Birthed through Trials

God sent me before you to preserve you as a remnant on
the earth and to save your lives by a great deliverance.
Therefore, it was not you who sent me here, but God,
who has made me a father to Pharaoh—lord of all his
household and ruler over all the land of Egypt.

—Genesis 45:7–8

God has given you an opportunity to become the vessel that will catapult your kin's financial future.

Today's Activity

Describe your company's products and services. In this section, list all your products and services. Describe the benefits your products and services offer your customer. Include pricing, product development, and if you have any patents on your product.

Pain Is Necessary
Pain Is a Reminder That You
Are Putting In Work

It is good for me that I have been afflicted;
that I might learn thy statutes.

—Psalm 119:71 (KJV)

Feeling growing pains? Good. You are expanding your territory. Pain is a motivator.

Today's Activity

Your marketing strategies. Market research is very important. As I mentioned before, carry out research on your competitors, whether online or on foot. Read what the information outlets are saying about your industry. List the barriers of entry. Barriers of entry are the difficulties involved with your market. List threats and opportunities.

Are there any coming changes that will affect your market? For example, changes in your field; changes in economy; changes in your local, state, or federal laws; and changes in technology. Will these changes help or become an obstacle for your business?

I recommend you take two or three days to complete a rough draft on this section, but do not fall behind. We have more work to do and you're almost there. Great job!

DAY 29

It's Okay to Cry, but It's Not Okay to Quit

For His anger *is but for* a moment, His favor *is for* life; Weeping may endure for a night, But joy *comes* in the morning. Now in my prosperity I said, "I shall never be moved."

—Psalm 30:5–6 (NKJV)

Today's Activity

Create a marketing budget. Use the affordability of social media. Literally hundreds of millions of people use social media daily. Take advantage of that. Create social media ads for your business. Make the ads quick and memorable. Social media outlets provide pricing for all budgets.

DAY 30

During the Summer, Plan for Winter

Idle hands make one poor, but diligent hands bring
riches. The son who gathers during summer is prudent;
the son who sleeps during harvest is disgraceful.

—Proverbs 10:4–5

Have you heard the story of the ant and the grasshopper? This was one of my favorite stories as a child. In this story, the ant worked hard to gather food. The grasshopper laughed at the ant's work ethic. The grasshopper was basking in the sun, enjoying the summer days. The grasshopper scoffed at the ant, but the ant was determined. The ant understood that the days will not always be sunny. Summer would not last forever. The grasshopper tried and incite the ant to quit its working and join him in slacking off, but the ant was focused.

You really need to analyze your relationship with people who are constantly inviting you to slack off. They are only concerned with the sunny days. They are not concerned about the future. They laugh at the prospect of owning your own business. Their agenda is all about leisure time. You need people around you who will push you to be better, those who will encourage you to reach further, and support you when you are at your lowest.

Take a survey of your inner circle. We need—we must—remove the grasshoppers from out intimate circle. It's not the time to slack off. It's the time to grind harder than ever. Sometimes our biggest distractions are the people around us. Yes, I believe if you work hard, you are entitled to play hard. But remember, you must work harder than you play.

Remove the people who distract you from getting to the finish line. The grasshopper did not take advantage of the harvest. Why do we believe that harvesttime is easy? We think that somehow the fruits will gather themselves and jump into the baskets and sell themselves. No, harvesttime is grinding time. You work hard planting, watering, waiting, trusting in your product. When harvest comes, it's time to gather the team, prepare the equipment, and gather the fruit. You have a small window to gather the good fruit. Once you gathered and sort out the good from the bad, it's time to go to market.

Hard work will always be part of the equation. Yes, you will get your well-earned leisure time, but let's not become negligent. The grasshopper ignored the fact that summer would not last forever. Winter was on its way. That's the thing about seasons—seasons will change, whether we plan for them or not. Project your vision further than the current situation. Work hard to build a nest egg; when funds are not coming in at their usual rate, you won't need to panic. Life will throw curveballs your way. Build a solid foundation.

When winter arrived, the grasshopper was unprepared. There was no fruit left to gather. Do not wait for situations to be at their worst to begin to plan. Be proactive. Be the ant in the story. Winter was a different situation for the ant. The ant planned, prepared, and executed. When you are the ant, the grasshoppers will come knocking at your door. Don't turn them down. Use it as a teaching moment and help them prepare for the changing seasons.

How can we prepare for winter? I believe the best way is to create multiple streams of income. "Don't put all your eggs in one basket," as the saying goes; if the basket breaks, so do your eggs. Diversification. Invest in stocks, mutual funds, open a high-yield savings account for emergency purposes only, and discipline yourself to save. Put a predetermined amount every week, biweekly or monthly, but maintain your savings schedule.

Owning your own business can secure your and your family's future. Isn't that something worth fighting for? You can establish a legacy that your love ones can follow for generations to come. You can become a standard of success within your family, friends, and community.

Today's Activity

Your distribution channels—map out your distribution channels. How are you going to get your product or service to your customers? Let's say, for example, you are selling baked goods out of your kitchen. Are your clients coming to you? Are you offering a delivery service? Are you shipping your baked goods to your customers? Maybe you are doing all three. Are you depending solely on word of mouth or are you using an e-commerce platform? Map it out. It's important to have a clear process to follow every time.

Don't Allow Anyone to Define You

Yet in all these things we are more than
conquerors through Him who loved us.

—Romans 8:37 (NKJV)

Who you are as an individual is not determined by others' personal opinions, but your actions will be judged. No matter how small your organization may be right now, you need an operational plan.

Today's Activity

Create an operations manual. Don't worry, we will keep it simple and yet elegant. Step one is simple. How do you create your products and/or deliver your services to your clients? Build a process that can be easily duplicated every time to maintain consistency. This is called quality control.

Who's part of your personnel? Probably it's all on you right now, but you will scale up and will need to hire. Research the legal climate of your business. Do you need licenses and certifications? Do you need insurance coverage or any specific regulations placed by your local, state, or federal governments in your industry?

Your business location might be your kitchen, living room, or an extra room in your home; but wherever it is, it must be in optimal condition to carry out your business. Do yourself a huge favor and keep the area organized. Keep a detailed inventory and a list of your suppliers, if needed.

Time to Go to War
Life Is the War,
Your Mind the Battlefield

Praise be to the LORD my Rock, who trains my
hands for war, my fingers for battle.

—Psalm 144:1 (NIV)

Today's Activity

Finalize your business plan. If you need further assistance, we are here for you. If you are doing some fundraising for your business, give your business plan a test run at a bank or an investor. Don't forget that your personal credit score is extremely important. Your credit score can be a major deciding factor in their decision in offering you a business loan or a line of credit. There are some companies that will offer you free credit report monitoring. Take advantage of these free services and check your credit score. Monitor your credit report, dispute any issues, and work to improve your score.

Conquer Fear

The LORD *is* on my side; I will not
fear. What can man do to me?

—Psalm 118:6 (NKJV)

The higher the risk, the higher the potential gain. Knowing when to take a risk and when to play it safe is an art that few can perfect. Analyze all the possibilities. Always keep in mind that there is a potential of financial loss in investments. Always have a safety net, in case the investment doesn't go as planned. Gradually increase the risk factor of your investments. Always make safe investments at the beginning until you learn how to manage risk and build a high-risk tolerance. Do your homework. Research, research, research. Always bet on yourself. You have the potential. Time to execute.

Today's Activity

Research two companies that you have considered investing in. Learn the difference between small-cap, mid-cap, and large-cap companies. Quick tip: The smaller the cap, the higher the potential to grow your investment but also the higher the risk. I recommend starting with mid-cap or large-cap companies. Small-cap companies are usually young companies. Mid cap and large cap are companies that have been around for a while, and even though the potential growth is smaller, the risk burden on your investment is lower.

DAY 34

You'll Get Them in Round Two

Though your beginning was small, yet your
latter end would increase abundantly.

—Job 8:7 (NKJV)

Do not allow failure to paralyze you. Not all business ideas will produce revenue. If an idea is hurting your initial vision, you have two options: reevaluate the idea or dump it all together. If it has not produced revenue and customers are not excited about it after three months, you may have to reevaluate or dump the idea.

Today's Activity

Acquire a small notebook or journal for your ideas. New ideas will come to you almost daily. Do not leave it to memory. Write these ideas down. You never know if one of those ideas will be the million-dollar idea. Refer to your notebook or journal at least once a month. This practice will be especially beneficial on the days when you lack inspiration or innovation. You already have the potential to be extremely successful within you. Now it's time to tap into it.

DAY 35

"I Start Counting When It Hurts"—Muhammad Ali

Stand firm, and you will win life.

—Luke 21:19 (NIV)

Being tired is never an excuse. The level of your determination will determine the level of your success. Let's take it to the next level. By now, exhaustion has probably kicked in. You probably thought it's time to take a break from it all. It's time to dig deep and get it done.

Today's Activity

Let's think about pricing. Are your products and services priced correctly? When it comes to pricing your products or services, you need to think about a few factors.

First, consider the cost. In detail, break down how much it costs to make the product. Don't leave one cent out of the equation. Include material cost, labor cost, time—do not leave anything out.

Second, consider the value of your product or service. What is a fair price for your product or service? What is your potential customer paying for a similar product from your competitors? Now consider your profit. Is the selling price enough to promote upscaling?

Remember, you need to be serious about your growth. Businesses that do not grow perish. If you have a product that is not selling, slash the price. Create a sale and move that inventory. You want to focus on the products and services that are selling and find ways to improve those products and services.

The Summit Is Near

"But as for you, be strong and do not give
up, for your work will be rewarded."

—2 Chronicles 15:7

The air is getting thinner. The higher you climb, the more difficult it is to breathe. The margin for error decreases. You must be mentally conditioned for the climb. Do not run away from challenges. Face them bravely. Formulate a plan and executed.

Today's Activity

Plan and execute a meet and greet for potential clients. Start with a small group, twenty people max. Show off your business. Highlight your key services and or products. Give them an opportunity to buy the product or service at a discounted price during the meet and greet.

During this activity, show your potential clients some love. Let them see why they should come to you and not your competitors. Create some buzz for your business. Show off your success. Share your vision to the world via your preferred social media outlets. Post pictures, short videos, etc.

DAY 37

You're a Phoenix—Rise from the Ashes

For the righteous falls seven times and rises again,
but the wicked stumble in times of calamity.

—Proverbs 24:16

I am fascinated by the legend of the phoenix, a mythological creature that rises from his ashes, full of wisdom and long life.

Today's Activity

Review your state's requirements once again. Make sure that you have all your licenses and/or permits in order. If you are selling retail goods, make sure you have the proper seller's permit from your state. The more you know, the better. Like the phoenix, you can rise from the ashes of desperation, and you and your business be blessed with long life.

DAY 38

You're Royalty, Humbly at the Top of the Food Chain

But you *are* a chosen generation, a royal priesthood, a holy nation,
His own special people, that you may proclaim the praises of
Him who called you out of darkness into His marvelous light.

—1 Peter 2:9

Carry yourself with dignity and pride. Be confident. Clients and investors can smell fear. Be fearless. Be proud of your hard work. Dress apart. First impressions are still a thing. Show up ready for business. Keep your appointments organized. Don't be late or on time—be early. Don't have the client waiting on you. You wait for the client. You are the most powerful marketing tool in your company's arsenal. Impress them with your professionalism every time. If you take yourself seriously, so will your potential clients.

Today's Activity

Review your local, state, and federal tax responsibilities. Yes, I know this is probably your least favorite thing, but get it done. You probably will hire a tax professional to file your taxes, unless you own a tax business. But it's important that you know your tax schedules as a safeguard.

A good idea is to obtain a small business tax calendar from the IRS. You can visit the IRS website for more information. It's imperative that you know every aspect of your business, even if you are outsourcing a responsibility.

DAY 39

Today Is a Good Day to Win

Then he said to them, "Go, eat of the fat, drink of
the sweet, and send portions to him who has nothing
prepared; for this day is holy to our Lord. Do not be
grieved, for the joy of the LORD is your strength."

—Nehemiah 8:10

Today's Activity

Develop or refine your personal and business budget. I cannot
stress how important it is to manage your debt. Find ways
where you can save money without compromising quality. You can
use a self-budgeting app, software, or the old-fashioned way of pen
and paper. Start with a simple budget. List all and prioritize your
expenses.

Tip: Once you have listed your expenses, contact the service
provider, vendor, or person and renegotiate the price. Contact the
cable company, cellphone company, insurance company, and any
other company where you purchase a product or service. You will be
pleasantly surprised at how many of these companies will work with
you to lower your bill. Companies prefer to negotiate with you rather
than lose your business to a competitor.

DAY 40

Prepare, Plan, and Execute

Now the angel of the LORD came up from Gilgal to
Bochim And he said, "I brought you up out of Egypt and
led you into the land which I have sworn to your fathers;
and I said, 'I will never break My covenant with you.'"

—Judges 2:1

In biblical numerology, the number 40 represents a determined time of trials, test, and desert experiences. You have stayed the course. Bravely face your trials. Take survey of where you are right now. There is no moment more important than now. By day 40, you have a good idea of what works and what doesn't. Prepare for your next big move. Think of what will bring your business to the next level. Plan for it. Write everything. List everything. Execute. Get it done. Failure is not trying. Failure is not taking a stance. You need to see the promised land closer now.

Today's Activity

Take a survey of your progress. What areas need improvement?
Reach out to us if you feel stuck.

Walk in the Counsel of the Wise

He who walks with wise men will be wise, but
the companion of fools will suffer harm.

—Proverbs 13:20 (NASB)

The number 41 is the number of coming out of the desert, coming out of trials, passing the test. You are about to enter your promised land. Not everyone around you can enter the promised land with you. Some have returned to Egypt—to the bondage of the mundane, to the bondage of the ordinary. Others have died in the desert. The promised land is on the other side of the river. What will you do? Will you stare at the body of water that stands in your way or will you jump into that sucker and start swimming? Let's go.

DAY 42

There Are No Shortcuts—This Road Is Paved with Hard Work

The soul of a lazy *man* desires and *has* nothing; but
the soul of the diligent shall be made rich.

—Proverbs 13:4 (NKJV)

See it through. No shortcuts. Get up early, go to sleep late. Sleep when you're done. Your work ethic needs to be your advantage. Be the hardest worker in the room. See it through.

DAY 43

You Are Building an Empire

The plans of the diligent lead to profit as
surely as haste leads to poverty.

—Proverbs 21:5 (NIV)

It's up to you to make it happen. Chances are, like me, you were not born into wealth. You were not given a silver spoon. You had to grind and hustle for yours. Well, that's okay. Thrones are one-seaters. That empire is meant for you to rule. Come on! You must build it, brick by brick, stone by stone.

How Would You Be Remembered?

The memory of the righteous *is* blessed, but
the name of the wicked will rot.

—Proverbs 10:7 (NKJV)

Think about legacy. Think about the footprints you will leave behind for generations to follow. The blueprints you will leave will lead your kin to achieve greatness. Do you want to be remembered as a subpar individual? Do you want to be remembered as someone who only gave 50 percent? Or do you want to be remembered as a man or woman on a mission, completely on beast mode. A trend setter. A visionary. A gift to humanity. It's up to you how you want to be remembered. Put in the work. Become a legend.

Do One More Repetition

But they that wait upon the LORD shall renew their strength;
they shall mount up with wings as eagles; they shall run,
and not be weary; and they shall walk, and not faint.

—Isaiah 40:31 (KJV)

One more repetition. Your muscles maybe lacking oxygen by now. Fatigue might have set in. Thoughts of slacking might be creeping in. What do you do? You do one more repetition. Just like in the gym. You must break through another plateau, reach another level. Tell yourself you'll rest when you are done, not when you are tired.

DAY 46

The Mentality of a Champion

Thou wilt keep him in perfect peace, whose mind
is stayed on thee: because he trusteth in thee.

—Isaiah 26:3 (KJV)

The goal is clear; the path has been laid. The summit is the goal, and hard work is the path. Greatness is the result. Anything else will be unacceptable. Champions hold themselves accountable. Champions will carry the team when necessary. Champions inspire their team to become better. Champions make their team better. We don't take no for an answer. Impossibility does not mean impossible; it just means we are working on the solution. Champions are relentless. Champions don't quit. Champions make no excuses. The mindset is set. Go big. Go strong. Never back down.

DAY 47

You Are an Eagle—Don't Share Your Vision with Pigeons

But those who hope in the LORD will renew their strength.
They will soar on wings like eagles; they will run and
not grow weary, they will walk and not be faint.

—Isaiah 40:31 (NIV)

Pigeons wait to be fed. They have fallen into this pattern of waiting for breadcrumbs. An eagle goes after his meal. An eagle sees an opportunity and takes it. An eagle goes for the kill. You are like an eagle—you see opportunity and you take it. No more waiting around to be handed a piece of bread. Execute! Take hold on opportunities.

Proverbs 4:25

Let your eyes look straight ahead; fix your
gaze directly before you.

The level of your hunger will determine the level of your success.

Give Back
Go Do Some Charity Work

> He who has pity on the poor
> lends to the LORD, and He will
> pay back what he has given.
>
> —Proverbs 19:16–18 (NKJV)

According to the article "9 Positive Effects of Donating Money to Charity" on www.thelifeyoucansave.org, these are nine benefits of giving back:

1. Experience More Pleasure

   In research conducted by the National Institutes of Health, participants who chose to donate a portion of $100 they were provided enjoyed activated pleasure centers in the brain. Although this experiment was controlled and scientific, it did show that donating money simply makes you feel better, which is something we can all benefit from.

2. Help Others in Need

We don't live in a perfect world, and there's never going to be a perfect time to give—but there are always people out there in need of help. Whether interest rates are rising, the economy is in the doldrums, or even if you're experiencing financial difficulties of your own, the reality is that when you donate your money, you help others who need it.

3. Get a Tax Deduction

If you give to an IRS-approved charity, you can write off donations on your tax return. Certain restrictions do apply, though. To learn more about them, along with whether or not a particular charity has IRS approval, check the IRS website or The Life You Can Save's fact sheet about tax deductibility. Donating your cash is a great way to reduce the amount of money you send off to Uncle Sam, and for a good cause, to boot.

4. Bring More Meaning to Your Life

When you donate money to charity, you create opportunities to meet new people who believe in the same causes that inspire you. That, and making a real impact on those causes, can infuse your everyday life with more meaning. If you've been stuck in a rut, whether personally or professionally, sometimes the simple act of donating cash can do the trick and reinvigorate your life.

5. Promote Generosity in Your Children

When your kids see you donating money, they're much more likely to adopt a giving mindset as they grow up. I write from personal experience. I've donated money to a variety of charities over the years and have always made sure to inform my eight-year-old son of my efforts. Last Christmas, when he and I were shopping at a mall, he spotted a kiosk for a charity and rather than spending some of his allotted money on Christmas gifts, he asked if we could sponsor a hungry child overseas. We signed up then and there. Do the same with your kids and you might see similar results.

6. Motivate Friends and Family

When you let your friends and family know of your charitable donations, they may find themselves more motivated to undertake their own efforts to give. It takes a village to address issues such as world poverty, scientific advancement, and early childhood education. Stoking passions in the folks around you is a very positive and tangible effect of your own giving.

7. Realize that Every Little Bit Helps

You don't need $10,000 to make a difference in someone's life. In developing countries, even just a few U.S. dollars could result in a week's worth of meals for a starving child, much-needed medical attention, and even improved schooling. Don't just think of your cash donation from an American economic perspective. Often that money can go a lot further elsewhere in the world.

8. Improve Personal Money Management

If you set a scheduled $100 donation each month for a particular charity, that can motivate you to be more attentive to your own finances in an effort to ensure you don't default or fall behind in your monthly donations. Anything that gets you to pay closer attention to your bank account is a good thing—especially when it helps those in need.

9. Give, If You Can't Volunteer

This might not necessarily be a positive effect of charitable giving, but if you're too busy to volunteer or otherwise donate your time, giving money is the perfect workaround. Never think that you can't improve someone's life or the world itself if your personal or professional schedule won't allow the time. Writing out a check is a simple way to show you're willing to help others in any way you can.

Today's Activity

Participate in a local charity event. This will give you a perspective on what is truly important. It will teach you appreciation for what you have and will give you the drive to work much harder. The wealth you are building today will be a bridge for many to cross. Remember, you are an instrument of blessing. Your fellow man is counting on you.

DAY 49

Water Your Plants

Sow your seed in the morning and do not be idle in the evening,
for you do not know whether morning or evening sowing
will succeed, or whether both of them alike will be good.

—Ecclesiastes 11:6

Don't ever ask an employee or team member to perform a task that you did not teach them to do. Water your people. Grow your people. Pour into your people. Talent is great, but it must be polished into a gift.

DAY 50

Accountability Time

Know well the condition of your flocks,
and pay attention to your herds.

—Proverbs 27:23

It's time to evaluate your progress.

Today's Activity

Make a list of the things your business is doing well. Have you created a process within your business—something duplicated over and over with ease and produces great results? Also, document the areas were improvements are required. List them by priority, and work on fixing them.

DAY 51

Find a Mentor

Iron sharpens iron, so one man sharpens another.

—Proverbs 27:17

You made it through the challenge. Time to work harder. Remember, getting to the top is hard, but staying at the top is harder. By now you probably have noticed that your inner circle is smaller.

Today's Activity

Find a good mentor who can continue to challenge you and bring the very best out of you. Link up with a business owner who is successful in your business field. Meet with your mentor at least once every two months. To become a teacher, you first need to be a disciple.

KEEP WORKING.

About the Author

Albert Cabrera, is CEO and founder of A&K Consultants NC, a motivational speaking firm. With over ten years of Christian leadership training, Albert Cabrera has help and encouraged countless individuals in sharpening their leadership skills. As a professor in the Theological International University, Albert has helped pastors and community leaders expand their visions. Using biblical principles and keen business sense, Albert has developed a blueprint for individuals to find the drive to take their dreams, passion, and/or ideas and transform them to a tangible, ever-expanding vision.

Albert Cabrera's desire is to see you become the best you, you can be. Born in the Dominican Republic and raised in New York City, he understands the difficult climb that is from the valley to the top of the mountain.